STOCKHOLM

STOCKHOLM
BEAUTY ON WATER

Distributed by:

Ultraförlaget AB

Svetsarvägen 18
Phone 46-8-983330 Fax 46-8-297550
S-17141 SOLNA
SWEDEN

Published and printed by

NARNI - TERNI

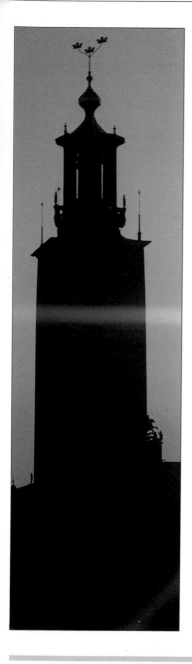

INDEX

STOCKHOLM:

Beauty between the water and the sky.

A visit to Stockholm is always a pleasant and stimulating experience for any traveller. In what is considered to be one of the most beautiful of Europe's capitals, it is particularly pleasant to stay during the summer period when the days are warm, and all the citizens come out on to the streets and enjoy the warmth of the sun -which has been a dream all through the long winter. The mild evenings are an invitation to wander romanticaly around the ancient heart of the city, in an atmosphere full of life and enjoyment. And in the winter, when the snow covers the whole city and the dominant colours are white and pale blue in a thousand different moonlit shades, Stockholm, encircled by thousands of lights, unveils its most enchanting aspect. This is especially so at Christmas, for which the Swedes have a particular feeling: coming out to make purchases in the small markets and the many little shops of the

centre is almost a ritual for the inhabitants of Stockholm, and no traveller can miss the fascination of this festive atmosphere which prevails everywhere in the city. The city landscape is very varied, and water plays a very important role in this because a third of the territory of Stockholm is in fact formed by water. Another third is occupied by the green of parks and woods, and only the final third is reserved for urban development. Because of this, the special quality of this city is that of a perfect mix of everything which serves to make a city something on a human scale.

Stockholm stretches between small bays, quays and narrow canals, having grown up on about fifteen islands which form part of an archipelago of something over 24,000. Each of the islands is linked to the others by bridges and tunnels, but in fact none is very far from the others, so that it is easy to get around, even on foot, and to make excursions which enable one to discover the history and traditions of this inimitable city.

SOME HISTORY

The official history of the city begins in 1252, the era to which the first document recording it as a fortified castle dates back. The castle was built on the orders of the governor, Birger Jarl, to protect the cities of Uppsala and Sigtuna from the ravages of the Estonians. Around the castle, the first nucleus of the city later developed, and it was then known as Stadsholmen - the city on the island. This area is known today as Gamla Stan, the old city. In time it became an important trading centre, thanks to its position between Lake Mälaren and the Baltic. In 1520 it was occupied by the Danish King, Christian, known as "The Cruel"; in fact he ordered the execution in the central square of the city of all those who opposed his government, in a day that from that time onwards was known as the Bloodbath. Recovery began with Gustav Vasa, King Gustav I, who engineered a rapid economic boom by his initiatives, and Stockholm was subsequently almost entirely rebuilt during the reigns of Gustavus Adolphus and Queen Christina. In the eighteenth century Stockholm assumed great importance in the cultural field, especially during the reign of Gustav III, a role which it seeks to go on maintaining even today, with a large number of cultural events such as exhibitions, shows and festivals which are held every year.

Stockholm is perhaps unique among the world's cities in that it is possible to bathe and fish everywhere, because there is no pollution, and the seas are clean and full of fish. There are in fact no heavy industries, and the environment is very carefully considered, a factor which makes this a very livable city.

Here the visitor can satisfy every need. From the cultural standpoint, Stockholm is one of those cities in which cultural and sporting events abound, and today they have also found an ideal site in the Globen Arena, a huge edifice with a futuristic appearance in spherical form, which houses the most important events of the city and which has already virtually become its symbol. The City Underground is also a symbol of the city and its love for the arts; with more than half its stations decorated by some of the world's most eccentric artists, it constitutes in itself the world's longest art gallery. But this is not all: in the city there are Museums for all tastes and all interests, and they have collections of great importance on show.

In the big parks of the city, a number of theatrical and musical events take place, together with dances, and folk music and dancing, especially on the occasion of the major traditional holidays, such as the Midsummer Festival or the Feast of St Lucia in December.

In the city it is possible to buy everything, but if you are looking for something typically

The limpid waters which wash the shores of Stockholm make it possible for anyone to fish calmly right in the centre of the city.

The traditional festivals are an important part of the city's life.
From top to bottom: the Feast of St.Lucia, the Midsummer Festival and the Stockholm Water Festival.

Swedish, we advise you to look out for the splendid crystalware typical of Swedish manufacture, or the delightful little wooden red ponies from Darlana. However, there will be no lack of ideas as you wander round the charming little shops of the Old City, or even the bigger commercial centres.

Night-life in Stockholm too is full of interesting surprises; to start with, the incredible number of restaurants of top quality, jazz clubs where many artists give live performances every night, and pubs which are especially prolific in the zone of Södermalm.

Stockholm, then, is a capital with a thousand faces and a thousand opportunities; exclusive yet within the range of anyone, modern and avant-garde but also respectful and proud of its own centuries-old cultural traditions. A city of everyone, and for everyone.

On this page and the previous one: Some views of the city, situated between Lake Mälaren and the Baltic.

GAMLA STAN

Gamla Stan is the old heart of Stockholm.

It is in fact the "Old City", the first nucleus of a town whose primary characteristic is that it is largely built on water. Stockholm stands on a series of islands, about fifteen in number, each linked to the other at various points. In particular, Gamla Stan quarter, on the island of Stadsholmen, is linked by five bridges to that of Norrmalm, in the more northerly part of the city.

The most ancient part of Stockholm began to take shape in the 13th century, becoming an important commercial meeting point, since its position half way between the Baltic and Lake Mälaren made it easy to reach; thus many government buildings were put up here.

This mediaeval quarter, wonderfully preserved, is made up of narrow little streets, ancient monasteries, fine facades from

A glimpse of the Old City (Gamla Stan), in an excellent state of conservation.

The characteristic, elaborate seventeenth and eighteenth century facades of the Old City.

the seventeenth and eighteenth centuries, copper roofs and historic buildings facing out on to the clear blue water of a sea which is absolutely unpolluted even in the city.

The picturesque heart of the Gamla Stan quarter is the **Stortoget** (The Great Palace), surrounded by the fine facades of the houses of nobles and merchants. The piazza is further beautified by an exquisite fountain, and on the northern side by the former Stock Exchange Building, the **Börhuset** (1778) which today houses the *Swedish Academy* and the *Nobel Library*.

This piazza was the scene of a particularly tragic event in the history of Sweden, for this is where King Christian II of Den-

mark ordered the massacre in 1520 of 82 Swedish nobles, among whom was the father of the future king, Gustav Vasa; they were opposed to the union of Sweden with the Danish Crown. This episode has passed into history as the "Bloodbath" of Stockholm. According to the legend, one of the facades of the houses which face on to the square is decorated by a number of tiles equal to the number of persons decapitated in this tragic episode.

Today Stortoget is one of the most evocative and animated corners of Stockholm. There are many pleasant open-air cafés, and in winter a traditional and very pretty Christmas market is held here.

CHRISTMAS IN STOCKHOLM

During the month of December, there is at least one special reason for visiting the city of Stockholm: the little Christmas markets. Many of them are held, in very different sites, such as in the open-air museum of Skansen, in the little islets surrounding the city, or in Gaml Stan. The market which is held i the main square of the old city i particularly charming; it has tra ditionally been held here sinc the XIV century, an age when th merchants were almost all Ger mans, Danes or Dutchmen. Bu in 1523, King Gustav Vasa, by

decree prohibited all foreign merchants from the market, thus ensuring that the merchandise on sale would be of exclusively Swedish manufacture. Ever since then, this market has kept the same style and the same atmosphere and to wander round the dozens of stalls is undoubtedly an excellent way of entering into the Christmas spirit. The Christmas market on Skansen is also very attractive. Here the craftsmen make the hundreds of articles designed to bring cheer and festivity to Christmas on the spot. The delightful decorations, typical of the Swedish Christ-

mas, shimmer on the richly decorated Christmas trees; a thousand candles light up the stalls and the whole is accompanied by cheerful popular tunes played by street musicians. During the Christmas period the atmosphere of the city is absolutely unique. Lights, songs, colours: everywhere the shopwindows are twinkling and decorated with special care. Every street and square is lit up, but if this is not already enough to persuade you to enter into the Christmas spirit, then stop for a moment in a fine typical restaurant; here you will find the *Julbord*, the Christmas variant of *smörgåsbord*, (the classic buffet of the Swedish cuisine), in which there are countless specialities of the local culinary tradition. Apart from the stronger dishes of the Swedish cuisine, such as *kåldomar* or *ärtsoppa*, *Julbord* also offers traditional Christmas delicacies, such as roast pork rib accompanied by good red cabbage, or roast pork, herring salad or the many tasty cooked meats. Try it for yourselves.

Christmas is one of the most popular festivals in the city and in the whole of Sweden: from decorations to food, everything is special and attention is paid to the minutest detail during the Christmas period.

THE RIKSDAGSHUSET

(PARLIAMENT HOUSE)

This dates from the late nineteenth century, and is to be found on a small island between the old city and the Norrmalm quarter. It was the seat of the old Parliament. Begun in 1888 to a design by Aron Johansson, it was completed around 1906. Initially the home of the Parliament which first had two Chambers and then was reduced to one, the imposing building can be visited free of charge in the summer, every day except Sunday. Since 1971 it has also been used for art exhibitions, as well as hosting numerous theatrical performances. Some years ago, when excavations were going on under the Parliament House for an underground carpark, a number of ar-

chaeological remains were discovered. The idea of a carpark was therefore abandoned, and in its place a **Museum** was set up, in which interesting finds and documents are on display, testifying to the important and ancient civil heritage of the city.

The elegant facade of the Parliament Building from the early years of the 20th century. On the page opposite, the entrance arch to the Parliament Building.

KUNGLIGA SLOTTET

(THE ROYAL PALACE)

This imposing building was re-built in the 18th century, on the ruins of the ancient mediaeval castle of the "Three Crowns", the remains of which can still be seen today in the part under-neath the Palace, in the **Slottsmuseum**, which tells the story of the various stages of construction of the castle. The rebuilding was originally the work of Nicodemus Tessin the Younger, called in by King Charles XII after the fire of 1697, but it was only completed in 1754, by his son Carl Gustaf Tessin and by Carl Hårleman.

The Palace, which is also re-ferred to as the Castle, is the product of various architectural styles, from the baroque to the roccoco and the Gustavian style, but even so it keeps a substan-tial harmony in proportions and structural lines. The plan is quadrangular, and it is preced-ed by another two symmetrical constructions which close in the broad central courtyard in which the traditional *Changing of the Guard* ceremony takes place.

In the interior, decorated with splendid furnishings, arrasses, porcelains and valuable tapes-tries, there are more than 600 rooms, among the most interest-ing being the *Room of the Columns* dating from 1730, the *Rooms of Queen Lovisa Ulrika* in which a valuable collection of Italian paintings is kept; the *Guard Room*, the *Bernadotte Gallery*, with its portraits of the Royal Family, and the *Apartments of King Oscar*, in the roccoco style. There is al-so the huge and famous *Ballroom*, known as *Vita Havet* (The White Sea) because of the colour of its walls. This is to be found inside the *Festvånigen* (Ceremonial Apartments). In the *Rikssalen* (Throne Room), which is a splendid example of Hårleman's architectural style, there is a ce-sellated silver throne from 1640. In the *Skattkammaren* (Treasury) the Crown Jewels are on display, among them a fine crown of Flemish workmanship dated 1561, which belonged to King Eric XIV. In the interior of the Palace, opposite the Throne Room, we find the *Slottskyrkan* (Castle Church), built by Carl Hårleman to a design by Nicodemus Tessin the Younger in the roccoco style, decorated with works by Bouchardon. The *Representationsvän* (State Apart-

The Royal Palace of Stockholm (Kungliga Slottet), formal residence of the royal family of Sweden, in the baroque style. In the interior there are more than six hundred rooms and interesting museums.

ments) are also open to the public. The furnishings are particularly beautiful and of fine workmanship, notably the Gobelin tapestries. In the northern wing of the Palace another Museum is housed: the **Gustav III Antikmuseum**, which contains some of the antiquities collected by King Gustav III, a keen enthusiast for art and archaeology. Another splendid Museum, which is also the oldest in Sweden, having been established in 1628, is the **Livrustkammaren**, near the Palace, which displays arms, royal carriages and Swedish costumes.

Kungliga Slottet is the biggest building in the world still to be used for its original purpose; in fact the King and Queen have their offices here; they receive in these rooms, and they hold state banquets here. Guests on official visits are also lodged in the Guest Rooms in the Palace. Opposite the South side of the Palace the **Slottsbacken** opens out; this is the square in which the statue of Gustav III stands. The work by J.T.Sergels is accompanied by an obelisk which records the faithfulness of the citizens to Gustav III in the war against Finland. Also in the same square is the **Finska kyrkan** which is situated in a fine late seventeenth century room, used once as a handball court. Among other churches, we should mention the **Tyska** **Kyrkan** (German Church), built to extend the Chapel of St Gertrude, a building dating from 1576. It was reconstructed in the first half of the seventeenth century in the baroque style, at the behest of a number of German merchants. The Church's most notable feature is a long and elegant copper spire; it has an elaborate interior with reticulated ceiling, which is embellished by a series of elaborate baroque German tapestries. In 1887, as a consequence of a fire, the fine bell-tower was rebuilt.

The traditional Changing of the Guard ceremony, which takes place in the Great Courtyard of the Royal Palace. On the page opposite, some of the sumptuous rooms of the Palace. Above, the room known as Vita Havet (White Sea), because of the pale colouring of its walls.

Above: *another richly decorated room in the Royal Palace.*
Below: *a winter image of the Kungsträdgården, once a garden reserved for the royal family alone.*

THE STOCKHOLM OF THE SWEDISH ROYAL FAMILY

The Swedish Royal family, made up at present of King Carl Gustav XVI, who came to the throne in 1973, and his gracious wife Queen Silvia, with Princess Victoria, Prince Carl Philip and Princess Maddalena, is one of the most ancient in the world. It is the third oldest royal family in Europe to reign without a break. The permanent residence of the royal family is in the palace of Drottningholm, a little way outside Stockholm, recently recognised by UNESCO in its list of representative historical monuments of 18th century European Architecture.

The Royal Palace, which is found in the city is one of the largest uninhabited royal palaces in the world, in which one can visit the Museums, and the splendidly furnished apartments. The Ceremony of the Changing of the Guard which is held daily in the external courtyard of the Palace, is an ancient tradition going back to 1523, the era in which Gustav Vasa was crowned in Stockholm. The Kungsträdgården is also linked to the Swedish royal family, as the name implies. In former times, from the 16th to the 18th centuries, only members of the royal family had access to the garden, which is now a public park. It was used to supply them with rare herbs.

Another important place to visit is the Vasa Museum, in which the richest and most powerful warship ever constructed is on exhibition, in a cleverly designed environment of copper and concrete, from which three masts sprout. The warship was made at the urgent request of the hero-king Gustavus Adolphus II in 1625, and its story is rich in tales and legends.

STORKYRKAN

(THE CATHEDRAL)

This is the oldest church in Stockholm. Records of it go back to 1279, but the building has been the subject of constant refurbishing and rebuilding, up to the most recent one at the hands of the architect J.E.Carlberg in the years 1736 and 1745, which added the fine bell-tower and clock to the building.

In the fifteenth century Cathedral, the crowning of all the Swedish sovereigns has taken place. The interior, divided into five naves, is in the Gothic style, and is a fine example of solemn elegance, with its reticulated ceiling, numerous tombs and its very famous wooden carved group in the left-hand nave portraying St George and the Dragon, the work of the Lubeck Master, Bernt Notke, who completed it at the end of the fifteenth century. It is considered to be one of the most valuable ancient sculptural groups in northern Europe. Also by the Lubeck master is the fine fifteenth century Crucifix to the right of the baptismal font, and the sumptuous tomb of De Lagardie.

Inside the church there is the oldest view of Stockholm in existence: this is the *Vädersoltavlan*, a magnificent landscape view of the city beneath the sun, dating back to the early years of the sixteenth century.

There are other important works in the Cathedral: we may just mention some scenes from *The Life of Christ*, a series of reliefs in stone from the city of Riga, of valuable workmanship, dating from the end of the sixteenth century, and the fine *pulpit*, built by B.B.Brecht to a design by Tessin the Younger. Among the most interesting tombs is that of Tessin himself, planned by Carl Milles in 1933, or that of Marshal Stenbock, also designed by Tessin, but this time realised by Bernard Fouquet.

The splendid wooden statue of St George and the Dragon *by Bernt Notke, inside the Storkyrkan. On the page opposite an external view of the Storkyrkan, Stockholm's Cathedral.*

RIDDARHUSET

(THE HOUSE OF THE KNIGHTS)

The **Riddarhustorget**, the square with the fine statue of Gustav Vasa by Pierre Hubert l'Archevêque in its centre, takes its name from the building which faces on to it. This is the **Riddarhuset**, one of the finest palaces in the whole city, in Dutch baroque style.

It was built in 1640-1674 to a design by Simon de la Vallée, completed by his son, Jean de la Vallée. The Renaissance façade, on the other hand, is the work of the Dutchman Joost Vinckboons, but also dates from the mid-seventeenth century. In this building all the Swedish nobility used to assemble, and the approximately 2000 coats of arms of the most important families of Sweden are now preserved in the numerous rooms of the Palace.

The House of the Knights (Riddarhuset) with the Statue of Gustav I Vasa.

RIDDARHOLMSKYRKAN

(CHURCH OF THE ISLAND OF THE KNIGHTS)

On Riddarholmen, the small island to the west of the old city, there is the ancient church which today houses the remains of many of the Swedish royalty, the **Riddarholmskyrkan.**

The Church faces out onto **Birger Jarl torg** the big square dedicated to the founder of the city, whose *statue* can be seen right at the centre of the square - a work by Fogelberg, dated 1854. The ancient structure of the Church of Riddarholm goes back to 1270, when a friary was built for the Franciscans, at the orders of King Magnus I Ladulås. The church underwent many restorations subsequently, but we know that the earliest building scheme, typically Francescan, was initially without towers. and with two naves. Some of the chapels were added in the fifteenth century. while the very high tower was built in 1846. Today the Church has triple naves, and is decorated with a large

Riddarholmen: the main church on the island of the Knights (Riddarholmskrykan).

number of coats of arms, trophies and flags of the Knights of the Seraphic Order. Many kings of Sweden are buried here. In the *Karolinska Gravkoret*, by Tessin the Elder, completed by Carl Hårleman in 1738-43, (among others) King Charles Gustav X, Charles XI, Charles XII are buried, as well as wives of the kings and some princes of the royal blood. The *Gustavianska Gravkoret* dates from 1633, and is a work of Jost Henne. Here we can find the sarcophagus of Gustavus Adolphus II, the Great Gustavus Adolphus IV, Gustavus III, and many other tombs in addition to those of the royal consorts. The *Bernadotteska Gravkoret* was built in 1858-60 by F.W.Scholander. Here the founder of the present dynasty, Charles XIV, Johan Bernadotte and his wife Desideria, King Oscar I and King Gustav V and their respective wives are all buried.

In the Birger Jarl Torg, on which stands the Church of the Knights'Island, is the statue which commemorates the city's founder, Birger Jarl.
Opposite: *the unmistakable outline of Stockholm City Hall.*

KUNGSHOLMEN

This large island, whose name means "Isle of the King" is characterised by the fine red brick palace of the **Stadshuset** (the City Hall), from which a splendid view can be had over the whole city spread out amid the waters. In this quarter, which is to the north-west of Gamla Stan, there is also the **Kungsholms kyrkan**, a fine church of late seventeenth century construction. The **Kronobergsparken** is a large green lung, right at the centre of the island, and the **Radhuset** is a building from the beginning of this century in Renaissance style, today used as a courthouse.

A glimpse of the Strandvägen, a gracious avenue between ancient mansions and fine shops facing on to the water.

Another two views of the city with its fine balance between tradition and modernity.

The Globen Arena is the largest spherical construction in the world, and today is considered one of the symbols of the city of Stockholm. It is the site of a series of prestigious annual events in the fields of culture, music and sport.

STADSHUSET

(THE CITY HALL)

This imposing building is surely one of Stockholm's symbols, with its red bricks and its tower surmounted by the carillon and a gilded weathercock modelled on the three crowns of the national arms.

High up at the sides of the tower, the gilded figures of St *George and the Dragon* can be seen moving at 12.00 and 18.00 of each day. The view of the city for anyone looking out from this tower, which is about 106 metres or 330

The fine tower of the City Hall is surmounted by a carillon and a gilded weather cock figuring the three crowns of the national coat of arms.

feet high, is unforgettable, and is one of the most celebrated views in the whole of Stockholm. Inside the tower there is a **Museum** in which there are interesting works of art from various periods.

The City Hall was built between 1911 and 1923 by Ragnar Öst-berg, an important exponent of the national romantic style, and the project was financed by popular subscription. It was inaugurated in June 1923, on the four hundredth anniversary of the enthronement of Gustavus Vasa, the first Swedish monarch. On the eastern side, beneath a

The exterior of the City Hall, from which one can obtain a splendid panorama of the city.

baldacchino, there is a statue of the founder of the city, Birger Jarl, in a monument in the form of a golden sarcophagus, the work of Sandberg.

Inside we find the Blå Hallen (The Blue Hall). In this room every year on 10th December, the traditional gala banquet is held to celebrate the award of the Nobel Prizes.

Another splendid great hall is the famous *Gyllene Salen* (Golden Hall), decorated with amazing gold mosaics formed from about 20 million pieces.

The impressive mosaic in the Golden Chamber (Gyllene Salen) of the City Hall of Stockholm. It portrays the ancient history of the city.

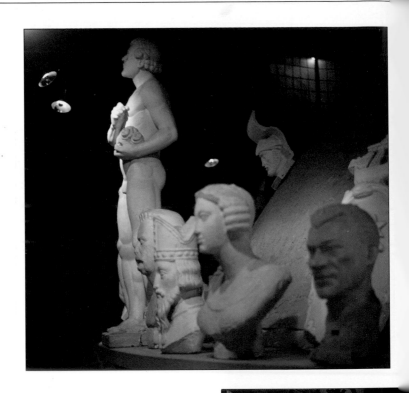

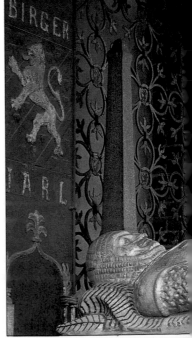

Above, in the Tower of the City Hall there is an interesting Museum with works of art from various ages and origins.
Opposite: The funeral monument of Birger Jarl, founder of the city, near the City Hall.

A typical view of the city which stands on a group of about fifteen islands, and is situated in an archipelago with more than twenty four thousand in all. We should remember that in the city

here is the first, and so far the largest, national park in the world within the confines of a city: this is the Ekoparken.

THE NOBEL PRIZE

Swedish cultural life, as well as cultural research all over the world is indissolubly linked to the name of **Alfred Nobel.**

A year before his death, in 1895, Nobel signed a will in which he declared that the greatest part of his patrimony should constitute an investment fund. The proceeds from this investment were to be, according to the actual words of his will.."*distributed annually in the form of a prize to those who have contributed, during the course of the year, to the wellbeing of humanity... whether Scandinavian or not*" Nobel sought in particular to promote five fields of activity: physics, chemistry, physiology or medicine, literature and the brotherhood of peoples (peace).

The task of assigning the prizes is entrusted to three Swedish insitutions and to a special Committee elected by the Norwegian parliament, since at that time Sweden and Norway were united in a single kingdom. Alfred Nobel had given to Norway the task of selecting the candidates for the Peace Prize, a responsibility which is still exercised by the same country.

On 10th December every year, the day of the anniversary of Nobel's death, the award of the prizes takes place contemporaneously in Stockholm, at the Konserthuset, and in Oslo, in the presence of the royal family.

NORRMALM

To the north of the old quarter of Gamla Stan there is the district of Norrmalm, which together with the former is considered the real heart of the city, with its fine squares, ancient churches, streets full of shops where everything can be found, and elegant cafés and restaurants.

The large **Gustav Adolf torg**, the square in front of the island where Gamla Stan is situated, is surely one of the most popular places in the city. Its present appearance is due to Nicodemus Tessin the Younger. In the centre is the equestrian *statue* of King Gustavus Adolphus II, the Great, a work by Pierre Hubert l'Archevêque, dated 1796. In the square itself, the building which now houses the Ministry of Foreign Affairs is of some interest : the **Arvfurstens Palatset**, completed in 1794, and formerly the residence of the Crown Prince. There is also the **Medelhavsmuseet** (Museum of the Mediterranean), a late 19th century building, where visitors can see objects witnessing to the cultural values of the ancient Mediterranean and Islamic civilisations. Further important

In the Gustav Adolf torg in the Norrmalm quarter stands the equestrian statue dedicated to king Gustavus Adolphus II, the Great.

The Stockholm Opera House, erected in 1890.

buildings are to be found in the vicinity of this square, beginning with the **Kungliga Opera** (Royal Opera House). Its present neo-baroque appearance was in fact the work of the architect Anderberg, at the end of the nineteenth century. The excellent cuisine of the famous *Operakälleren*, one of Stockholm's most renowned restaurants, should not be missed. Not far away is the **Kungsträdgården,** a very beautiful square surrounded with trees and enlivened by the young and old; once it was a garden reserved exclusively for the royal family. Here is the **Sverigehuset**, the home of the Tourist Office and of the bookstore of the Swedish Institute.

In the southern part of the quarter, opposite the small island of Skeppsholmen, there is the **National Museum**, with the most important art collection in the country. This is a building in the Renaissance style, but erected in 1866, designed by the German architect, Stüler.

Some views of Kungsträdgården.

49

NATIONAL MUSEUM

On the first floor it has splendid collections of arrasses from Brussels, Tournai, and Oudenarde; a series of Italian ceramics from the 15th and 16th centuries and many other artworks of great value, including the coronation robe of Gustavus Adolphus II, and an Italian polychrome relief of the end of the 15th century, portraying a Deposition. On the second floor in the numerous exhibition rooms there are splendid collections of Italian paintings and sculpture (with

works by Bronzino, Giambellino, Veronese, Tiepolo and Canaletto, to name the most famous), and Spanish artists such as Goya, El Greco or Ribera.

Room 307 should also not be missed, with its superb portraits by Rembrandt, various paintings by Rubens, Van Dyck and Brueghel. Among the French artists represented, we should mention Delacroix, Géricault, and Renoir, Monet and Pissarro among the Impressionists.

There are also works by Cézanne, Toulouse-Lautrec and Gauguin.

The Norrmalm Quarter is also the capital's "City" quarter, with modern and avant-garde buildings. Among these is the **Kulturhuset** by Peter Calsing, who built it between 1966 and 1970 - a Cultural Centre with exhibition rooms, theatres, conference halls and a library. The quarter on which this building looks out is the central **Sergels torg,** the name of which commemorates one of the most famous Swedish sculptors, Johan Tobias Sergels, who lived from 1740 to 1814. At the centre of the square is a modern *fountain* in crystal, by Edvin Öström, dated 1974. From this square the most modern area of the city begins: on the **Sveavägen**, in fact, we find the five skyscrapers which mark the beginning of the modern development of the city from the 1950s onwards. Near this street, which is particularly avant-garde architecturally, the zone of **Sergelgatan** is situated, leading towards the **Hötorget,** a square where a very colourful fruit and vegetable market is held. facing on to the square stands the **Konserthuset** (Concert Hall), in which each year the ceremony of the presentation of the Nobel Prizes takes place. The building is the work of Ivar Tengbom, built in 1926. In front of this building is the lovely *Fountain of Orpheus* by Carl Milles, designed in 1936. The adjacent **Kungsgatan** is one of the most important commercial thoroughfares in Stockholm, along which can be found the two **Kungstornen** (Royal Towers), the most ancient "skyscrapers" of the city (1926), each one 16 storeys high. Among the churches of this area, mention should be made of the

The multicoloured fruit and vegetable market in the Hörtorget.

Jacobs kyrkan of 1643, in late Gothic style, with three naves and baroque furnishings, and of the **Santa Klara kyrkan**, characterised by a very high tower by C F Adelkranz. It dates back to 1280, the year in which it was built as a nunnery, but it was completely rebuilt in the eighteenth century. There is also the **Adolf Fredriks kyrkan**, dated 1774 and built to a design by C.F.Adelcranz, in late baroque style. Inside there is an interesting altarpiece, figuring the Resurrection, and the E*pitaph of Descartes*, the famous French philosopher, who died in Stockholm in 1650. In the nearby cemetery the painter J.T.Sergels and Olof Palme, the Swedish Prime Minister who was assassinated on the Sveavägen in 1986 are both buried.

The Fountain of Orpheus by Carl Milles, opposite the Konserthuset.

THE STOCKHOLM UNDERGROUND:

THE WORLD'S LONGEST ART GALLERY

The 108 kilometres making up the underground network of Stockholm form the unusual background for one of the most incredible art collections in the world. Inside at least half of the stations of the Underground there are sculptures, paintings, frescoes, murals and every other kind of expression of the creativity and the eccentricity of hundreds of artists who have contributed, year by year, to the enriching of this uniquely amazing exhibition.

Every year the city administration spends about two million krone for the maintenance and new acquisitions of the collection. The idea of decorating the underground area which houses the Metropolitan lines was launched in the 1940s, when the first of these lines was built. From then onwards, more than 100 artists have contributed to giving form and colour and life to the stations. Among the most attractive to visit are the enttrance to Ar*senalsgatan* near Kungsträdgården, where an attempt has been made to recreate a classical environment, with statues, columns, paintings and plants. Then there is the famous T-Central Station, the arches of which are decorated with large garlands of blue leaves. In any case, all you need to do is take any line of the Underground, and get off where the decorations and the artworks on display seem most interesting. There really is something for every taste!

Two of the most colourful stations of the Stockholm Metropolitan Underground.

An excellent way of seeing the city is to take a tour by boat. The possibilities are infinite, since Stockholm stands on so many islands.

SKEPPSHOLMEN

This is the Little Island of the Ships: this is the meaning of the name, for in former times it was the base of the Swedish naval fleet.

This island, which is to day one of the favourite places of the inhabitants of Stockholm for their quiet walks in the green parkland, has a series of interesting museums.

These are the **Moderna Museet** and the **Photographic Museum**, which both display art and photography of Swedish and international artists of the 20th century. Among the paintings, we should mention works by Munch, Matisse, Léger and Picasso. There is also the **Architectural Museum**, concerned with both Swedish and international architecture, and the **Östaslatiska Museum**, an exhibition of ceramics from China, Japan, Korea and India.

Moored at the western side of the islet is an elegant white sailing ship: this is the *Chapman*, an English sailing boat from 1887, which is now the unusual and original site of the Youth Hostel.

The Isle of the Ships (Skeppsholmen): the nineteenth century clipper Af Chapman, now the home of a Youth Hostel.

On Skeppsholmen we find the Modern Art Museum, which has an interesting collection of works by Swedish and international artists of the 20th century, both inside the building and in the grounds.

ÖSTERMALM

This is the eastern quarter of the city, a modern and residential area. Here too we can find some museums, such as the **Historical Museum**, the Historiska Museet. The building which houses it dates from the thirties.

Historiska Museet In the Museum one of the most significant collections of prehistoric jewellery in the world in gold and silver is on display. There are around 2000 pieces in all in the collection, in a space dug out beneath the floor of the Museum, known as the Golden Room, opened to the public in 1994. There are unique specimen. from the 5th and 6th centuries BC such as necklaces, bracelets, pendant. and medallions. We know that the Vikings did not coin money, but divided their ornaments into small parts and used them for cash transactions. Many of these precious objects were discovered in the last century, in the land of a few farms whose owners, once they had found them, conscientiously handed them over to the state. In the Golden Room, the first item acquired by the Museum is still on display: this is a piece which formed part of the war booty of Gustavus Adolphus II, a reliquary of the 13th century.

The showpiece of the quarter, hidden away in the greenery of the **Humlegården**, is the **Kungliga Biblioteket** (The Royal Library). The building dates from 1871-1878, and it was then extended to house more than a million valuable volumes and thousands of manuscripts. Among these is the celebrated *Codex Aureus*, an ancient Gospelbook from the 7th century.

Not far from the Library is the fine **Engelsbrekts kyrkan** a church in the northern version of the Liberty style, the *Jugendstil*, built in 1914 by Wahlman. The main square of the quarter of Östermalm is the **Östermalmstorg**, on which stands the **Hedwig Eleonora Kyrkan**. The building of the church was first begun on the basis of a project by Jean de la Vallée in 1669, but it was completed much later by Adelcrantz, in 1737. The Church has a central plan and is surmounted by a large dome. Near this church is the **Kungliga Armémuseum** (Royal Military Museum), housed in a barracks dated 1763, where there is a large collection of arms and uniforms of the 16th century, and where the history of the Swedish army is given an overall review.

DJURGÅRDEN

On the large island of Djurgården, or rather Södra Djurgården, formerly the hunting reserve of the Swedish royal family and now a big public park, the oldest open-air museum in the world, the **Skansen**, has been set up.

Created in 1891, this museum houses more than 150 ancient houses and public buildings from many different parts of the country, which have been faithfully reconstructed here.

It was the ethnologist Artur Hazelius who had the idea of rebuilding whole villages to show the people of Stockholm how life and work were carried on in the various regions of Sweden. He bought up some farms which he then had dismantled and re-

---

Skansen keeps Swedish popular folk tradition alive. During the year, the atmosphere of popular festivals is recreated here, and there are constant evocative musical events.

built in this great park, after surrounding them with the flora and fauna typical of their places of origin, and peopling them with the same families. Among the first buildings on show was a farm from Dalarna, and a camp from Lapland.

Today there are also windmills, granaries, churches, shops and houses on display, representing various eras and social classes, and originating from all over the country. Through the inhabitants of these villages it is possible to take an active part in their daily life and the festivals which used to be held in days gone by, so that throughout the year one can relive the atmosphere of past traditions in this place.

Another important city museum is also to be found on this island: the most-frequented of all Swedish museums, in fact, the **Vasamuseet** (Vasa Museum) in which the pride of the Swedish Navy, the flagship Vasa is visible in all its splendour, after having been recovered from the sea bed where it sunk shortly after its launch in 1628.

The reconstruction of the villages of the various provinces of Sweden includes the old houses, the farms, churches and artisan workshops. Here the ancient popular traditions are kept alive.

VASAMUSEET

This Museum, inaugurated in 1900, is absolutely unique of its kind. It is a cavern made out of concrete, copper, glass and iron, from which the ship's masts emerge; it is subtly lit to show up the smallest details of the finest ghost ship ever found on the bed of the Scandinavian sea.

In 1628 this ship was urgently required by King Gustavus Adolphus II, who wanted to make it the most powerful warship in Scandinavia. Unfortunately, shortly after it began its maiden voyage, it began to list dangerously, and eventually sank to the bottom of the sea. Its excessive weight and disproportionate height were the causes of the disaster. Salvaged in 1961, the ship proved to have been very well-preserved because of the low salinity of the local seas, and a careful restoration gave it back to the Swedish nation as an invaluable reminder of the art of sailing in that era. Every year millions of visitors roam the gangways which run along the seven decks to examine every detail of the ship throughout its length (69 metres - 225 feet)

Recently the museum has been added to by another important find: this is one of the original sails of the Vasa, the oldest in the world, and the smallest of the six that were recovered. This is to be seen in the gallery on the seventh deck.

The Vasamuseet is not the only museum of this area: among others are the **Nordiska Museet** (Nordic Museum), in which the life and work of the Swedes over the last 500 years is illustrated.

In this very fine setting we also find some elegant residences and villas set amid the greenery, such as the **Prins Eugens Waldemarsudde**, a villa from the first years of this century in the *Jugendstil*, inhabited by Prince Eugene, who was famous for his skill as a painter. Inside this very elegant residence the original furnishings can still be seen, and a valuable collection of contemporary art works, both Swedish and foreign. Another splendid villa is the **Rosendals slott** of Fredrik Blom (1823-27), today a residential museum which commemorates its original owner, King Charles XIV Johan Bernadotte, who made it his summer residence in the first part of the nineteenth century.

On Djurgården there is also the open-air entertainment park **Gröna Lunds Tivoli**, very popular with adults and children. Here, as well as having fun on the numerous attractions, you can visit the circus or see exhibitions which are constantly changing.

The imposing hulk of the sailing ship Vasa.

The Vasa Museum is one of the most popular in Sweden. Recently it has been added to by further va

some of the original sails from the vessel, the oldest which have ever been found surviving whole.

Some details of the sailing ship Vasa which re-
mained submerged for more than 300 years on
the bed of the Baltic. The low salinity of the sea
preserved the structure of the ship and the elaborate details of its decoration.

Another detail of the Vasa
Museum.

The building of the Nordiska Museet on the island of Djurgården. Here the story of Swedish civilisation from the 16th century to the present is recorded.

SÖDERMALM

This is the southern quarter of the city, and is still an island, linked to Gamla Stan by an elaborate bridge, the **Slussen**. It was built by making use of a lock of 1637, which was supposed to serve to overcome the difference in level between Lake Mälaren and the Gulf of Saltsjön. The lock was later reconstructed in 1931, when it was widened and two lateral bridges were added, and later again it became possible to cross by the use of underground roads. In the central square of this thickly populated quarter, **Södermalmstorg**, one can climb up to the panoramic viewpoint of **Katarinahissen** to enjoy a splendid view over the city, or visit the **Stockholm City Museum**, in a fine building by Nicodemus Tessin the Elder, dating from 1680. The museum tells the story of this ancient city by using images and finds. Not far from the museum is the beautiful **Katarina kyrkan**, the work of Jean de la Vallée, completed in 1690. In the north-western part of the quarter there are still delightful little streets flanked by houses painted red, such as **Fjällgatan**. But in the eighteenth century, this street was a lot less pleasant and tranquil, since it was the place where the executions took place, and was thus called "Gallows Lane". The official executioner lived near here, in a house with a charming little garden, in what was then called Mikaels Tropp gatan - the nickname by which the executioner was known. Today it is known as **Sister Styverns gränd.**

A typical glimpse of the Södermalm district.

THE ENVIRONS OF STOCKHOLM

Stockholm is certainly a city of a thousand resources and surprises, but if we feel like moving out of it a little way, the surrounding area also has much to offer a visitor.

Among the various excursions which can be undertaken, we would mention these:

THE PALACE OF DROTTNINGHOLM

The residence of the Swedish Royal Family.

It dates from the seventeenth century, and its style is a pleasing blend of the baroque and the Gustavian.

It has been compared for richness and elegance to the Palace of Versailles.

A visit should include the Chinese Pavilion and the Palace Theatre, where splendid concerts and opera performances are held during the summer.

On this page and the previous one: *some views of the Palace of Drottningholm.*
Situated on the island of Lövon, on Lake Mälaren, it can be reached by leaving from the City Hall bridge by boat. A sight not to be missed is the wooden theatre dated 1766, in a fine state of preservation, and the Theatre Museum, where valuable old costumes and some original stage sets are preserved.

MILLESGÅRDEN

On Lidingö, a small island in the Archipelago opposite Stockholm, one can visit the fine house of the sculptor Carl Milles, nicknamed the Bernini of the North. Here, alongside the house there is an impressive collection of the artist's sculptures, graeco-roman in inspiration. The interior of the house is decorated with mosaics recalling the famous ones in Pompeii. In 1936 the artist gave the house, park and sculptures to the nation, so that this place should be constantly open to all, and also host works by other artists.

Some of the works by Milles displayed in the artist's fine house. In the interior of the house, in the "music room" the organ belonging to Leopold Mozart, father of Wolfgang Amadeus, is kept, and there are artworks by Canaletto, Donatello, Pissarro and Utrillo.

SKÄRGÅRDEN

This is the Swedish name of the Archipelago which lies immediately in front of Stockholm. There are more than 25000 islands and rocks rising from an unpolluted sea which is the delight of sailing enthusiasts.

Among the little towns of the archipelago we should mention Vaxholm, a settlement going back to the 16th century, and Dalarö with its simple fishermens' houses and its fine dwellings with mansards decorated with the thousand lacy interweavings of carved woodwork.

One Swedish family in three owns a boat; thus it is easy for them to reach their second homes in one of the islands in the archipelago by this popular means of transport; one can also spend time fishing or sailing. These are in fact the most popular activities among those who visit the archipelago, with its 24000 islands covered with all types of vegetation, sometimes low-growing and variegated and at other times woody and rich in mushrooms, blueberries and strawberries. The islands are a paradise for nature and sea lovers.

HAGAPARKEN

This is a natural park which lies on the western shore of the Gulf of Brunnsviken. It was commissioned and created by Gustav III at the end of the eighteenth century. The Pavilion of King Gustav in the park should not be missed; by Tempelman, it is in the celebrated Gustavian style. There are also the Kopparltälten, three great copper tents, and the House of the Butterfly, the Fjärilshuset.

TYRESTA NATIONAL PARK

About 20 km from the city, there is a huge forest of virgin pines, whose rocky territory opens up into a breathtaking valley, today the home of a very popular national park.

Strolling in the green countryside is certainly a good way to soak up the atmosphere pf Sweden, and everywhere there are parks and green spaces open to everyone.

But in the environs of Stockholm, there are truly countless opportunities to enjoy the greenery, or visit interesting places. Among the most popular places to visit, we should mention the Castle of Gripsholm in Mariefred on Lake Mälaren, the many-coloured town of Trosa in the Södermanland, the Viking Birka, or the interesting runic stones of Sigtuna.

PLACES OF INTEREST, MUSEUMS AND CASTLES OF STOCKHOLM AND ITS ENVIRONS

AQUARIA VATTENMUSEUM
Rain forests, piranhas, oceanic environments and coral reefs. A natural environment of the North, with mountain lakes and rapids.
Djurgården (between the Vass Museum and Gröna Lund). Tel. 6604940, Bus 44,47, Konsthallen.

ARKITEKTURMUSEET
Exhibition of Swedish and international architecture.
Skeppsholmen. Tel. 4630500 Bus 65. Kungaträdgårdan.

ARMÉMUSEUM
The history of the Swedish Army.
Riddargatan 13. Tel. 7889560

BERGIANSKA BOTANISKA TRÄRÄDGÅRDEN
Botanical Garden and Park
Frescati, Tel.156545 Bus 40 (T) Universitetet + bus 540

BIOLOGISKA MUSEET
Nordic animals
Djurgården Tel.4428215 Buss 44, 47, to Hazeliusporten.

COSMONOVA
Films on Maxi-screen and exhibitions on planetary and space themes.
Frescativägen 40 Te. 665130 (T) Universitetet or bus 40/540 Information 24 hours a day.
08-4570090

DROTTNINGHOLMS SLOTT
Residence of the Swedish Royal Family.
Ekerö, Tel. 75903 10 (T) Brommaplan + bus 301-323 Boat from the City Hall.

DROTTNINGHOLMS SLOTTSTEATER AND THEATRE MUSEUM
The Theatre of the Royal Residence, dating from 1766, with the original machines and decorations of the stage, plus an exhibition. *Tel. 7590406*

FOLKENS MUSEUM ETNOGRAFISKA
Collections and permanent exhibitions of various European cultures.
Djurgårdsbrunnsvågen 34

Tel.6665000, bus 69.

GRIPSHOLMS SLOTT
16th century castle with a National Portrait Gallery and Court Theatre.
Måriefred Tel.0159-10194 45 mins. by car/bus on E20

HISTORISKA MUSEET
Collection of objects and finds from the Viking Age and prehistoric period. Viking jewellery in gold and silver.
Narvavägen 13-17, Tel. 7839400 Bus 44,47,54 (Karlaplan) 56.76.69 Djurgårdsbron/Historiska museet. (T) Karlaplan or Östermalmstorg.

KAKNÄSTORNET
The tallest building in Scandinavia: 155 metres high (480 feet), 360°panorama over the city. *Lagudåsgärdet, Tel.6678030, Bus 69.*

KINA SLOTT
A Chinese pavilion erected for Queen Lovisa Ulrika in the second half of the eighteenth century.
At present it has been included in the list of world artistic heritage monuments.
Drottningholm Tel. 7590207

KULTURHUSET
Exhibitions, music, theatre, library, crerative activities.
Serges torg 3. Tel. 7000100.

KUNGLIGA HOVSTALLET
Museum of the royal carriages, horses and uniforms used on state occasions.
Väpnargatan 1, Tel.7898564. Bus 47,62 (T). Östermalmstorg.

KUNGLIGA SLOTTET
The Royal Palace and official seat of the Royal Family of Sweden. Royal Apartments, Bernadotte Apartments and Guest Rooms.
Tel. 7898500 Bus 43,46,55,59,76. (T) Gamla Stan.

LIVRUSTKAMMAREN
Armour, coronation robes and royal carriages, housed in a building of the Royal Palace.
Slottsbacken 3. Tel. 6664475, Bus 43, 46, 55, 59,76 (T) Gamla Stan.

MEDELHAVSMUSEET
Museum of Mediterranean civilisation and Islamic Art.
Fredsgatan 2, Tel.7839400
Bus 46, 48, 53, 59,62,65.
(T) Kungsträdgården.

MILLESGÅRDEN
The house, works and art collections of Carl Milles.
Carl Milles väg 2, Lidingö. Tel.7315060
(T) Ropsten - train to Torsvik.

MODERNA MUSEET
Swedish and international Art of the 20th century: paintings, sculpture and photographic exhibitions *Birger Jarlsgatan 57, Tel.6664259 Bus 46 (T) Rådmansgatan*

NATIONAL MUSEUM
Paintings and sculptures of the greatest international masters, drawings, graphic art and applied art. *Blasieholmskajen*
Tel. 6664250 Bus 65, 46, 62, 76
(T) Kungsträdgården.

NATURHISTORISKA RIKSMUSEET
Museum of natural history with special attention to the polar regions.
Frescativägen 40, Tel. 6664040
Bus to Riksmuseet or (T)
Universitetet.

NORDISKA MUSEET
The last 500 years of Swedish life. *Djurgårdsvägen, 6-16 (vid Djurgardsbron) Tel. 6664600.*
Bus 44,47,69.

RIDDARHUSET
House of the Nobility with 2325 heraldic coats of arms.
Riddarhustorget 10, Tel. 100857
(T) Gamla Stan.

RIKSDASGHUSET
The Swedish Parliament
Riksgatan 3A, Tel.7864000
(T) Gamla Stan.

SKANSEN
The oldest open air museum in the world.
Djurgården, Tel. 4428000, Bus 47,44.

SKATTKAMMAREN
The Treasure of the Royal House of Sweden *Royal Palace, Slottsbacken.*

Tel. 7898500, Bus 43,46,55,59,76.
(T) Gamla Stan.

SKOLOSTER SLOTT
Baroque castle about 70 km from Stockholm.
Bålsta Tel. 018-386077.
By Car: E 18 towards Enköping.
Train to Bålsta + bus 894.
Boats from the City Hall in the summer.

STADSHUSET
The City Hall, in which certain ceremonies of the Nobel Prize awards take place.
Hantverksgatan 1, Tel. 7859074
Bus 48, 62. (T) T-centralen, Rådhuset

STOCKHOLM GLOBE ARENA
The biggest spherical building in the world.
Sporting and musical events are held here.
Globen City, Tel. 7251000
(T) Globen.

TEKNISKA MUSEET
Swedish industrial and technological history.
Museivägen 7. Tel. 6631085, Bus 69
Teknorama Science Centre.

TOBAKSMUSEET
Museum of Tobacco, with exhibitions and a tobacco factory.
Gubbhyllan, Skansen, Tel. 4428026.
Bus 47, 44.

ULRIKSDALS SLOTT
The former palace of King Gustav Adolph VI and Queen Lovisa.
Bergshamra Solna, Tel. 850556
(T) Bergshamra + Bus 540
Queen Christina's coronation carriage at Ulriksdal Stables.

VASAMUSEET
The 1628 sailing ship recovered from the waters in front of the city. *Galärvarvet, Djurgården Tel. 6664800 Bus 47, 44, 69.*

ÖSTASIATISKA MUSEET
Ceramics, paintings and sculptures of China, Japan, Korea and India.
Skeppsholmen, Tel. 6664250
Bus 65,46, 62, 76.
(T) Kungsträdgården.

STOCKHOLM INFORMATION SERVICE

Sverigehuset, Hamng. 27, PO Box 7542, 103 93 Stockholm
Administration: 7892400
Fax: 7892450
Tourist Centre, Sverigehuset, Tourist Information 7892490
Excursion Shop, Sverigehuset
(Tickets and bookings) 7892415
(Guide-arrangements) 7892496

Tourist Centre and Excursion Shop . . . . Fax 7892491
Hotel Centre, Central Station
(Hotel-booking) . . . . .240880 - Fax 7918666
Kaknäs Tower, Gärdet
(Tourist Information) . . . . .7892435 - 6678030 - Fax 6678507
"The Sweden Shop", Sverigehuset, Hamngatan 27 (Souvenir) 7892406
Events information 0712-30100
Summer-open Tourist Informations:
The City Hall Tourist Information and Info Stop, Stockholm at Scandic
Hotel, Kungens Kurva.

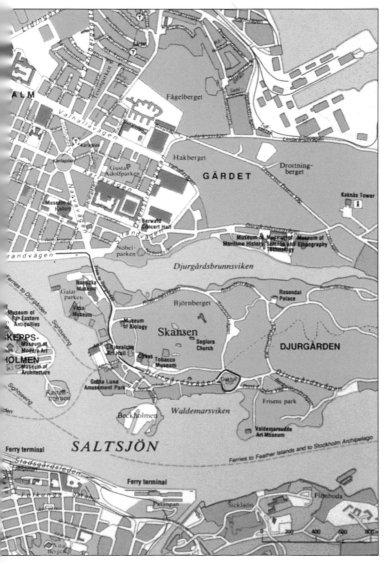

TUNNELBANA - METRO

TEXT: Stefania Belloni

PHOTOGRAPHS:

Archivio Plurigraf
Hans Hammarskiöld for the Vasa Museum: pages 69, 70, 72, 76, 77.
Historiska Museet: page 64.
Rolf Nyström: pages 4, 7, 19, 34, 42, 60.
Ente Svedese di Milano: pages 14, 17, 24/2, 57/1, 80, 85/2, 88/1, 90, 94.
Marie Andersson: page 68/1.
Dan Larsson: pages 66, 68/2.
Focus Team: pages 16, 26.
Ultraförlaget: pages 10, 25, 44, 58, 82, 89/2.